COMMONPLA(

Taylor Strickland is a poet and translator from the US. He is the author of *Commonplace Book* and *Dastram/Delirium*, his forthcoming versions of Alasdair Mac Mhaighstir Alasdair (both with Broken Sleep Books). Recently, his poem 'The Low Road' was adapted by American composer, Andrew Kohn, and performed in Orkney. His poem 'Nine Whales, Tiree' is in the process of being adapted to film with filmmaker Olivia Booker and composer Fee Blumenthaler. He is currently a doctoral candidate in literary translation at the University of Glasgow, and he lives in Glasgow, with his wife, Lauren.

The poems of Commonplace Book search for promise and light in disillusionment, but are aware that brilliance doesn't preclude abandonment: they are powerful explorations of the complications and limits of the marvellous.

— Pàdraig MacAoidh/Peter Mackay, *Gu Leòr / Galore*

The poems in Commonplace Book are sonically-attuned, troubled, poised between joy and loss, heaven and earth. Taylor Strickland's work brings us right into the landscapes of Scotland and of the mind, drenching us with rain, then breaking us open with a warm, forgiving sun.

— Seán Hewitt, *All Down Darkness Wide*

Taylor Strickland's Commonplace Book finds a common place for the common and uncommon, for CalMac ferries and Alasdair Mac Mhaighstir Alasdair's 'Birlinn of Clanranald', for Alba and Jessica Alba, for the modern office and abandoned Highlands landscapes. Strickland is a deft poetic geographer, following desire paths across continents and sketching starkly memorable studies of the American mid-west and the Scottish North Atlantic. As a connector of cultures, he knows that 'Love is a hyphen', but follows an underlying elegiac itch in search of the 'Never-green, a nothing-nest, /so eerily similar to nothingness' – eerily similar, yet richly present and sustaining too.

— David Wheatley, *Stravaig*

A pamphlet of rare music. I loved it

— Niall Campbell, *Noctuary*

Taylor Strickland's verse explores the natural world that exists in a huge variety of places, ranging from the Great Lakes of the United States to the tiny island of Tiree off the west coast of Scotland, touching on the myths and legends that are part of the history of these locations on his way. He does this with excellence and style, revealing much about the workings of his own heart and mind as he does so. An outstanding poet, his every word displays the range of his craft and mastery.

— Donald S. Murray, *In a Veil of Mist*

Contents

ISBN: 978-1-915079-45-9

Cover designed by Aaron Kent

Edited & Typeset by Aaron Kent

Broken Sleep Books Ltd   Broken Sleep Books Ltd
Rhydwen   Fair View
Talgarreg   St Georges Road
Ceredigion   Cornwall
SA44 4HB   PL26 7YH

Commonplace Book

Taylor Strickland

because place calls to place
inside us
- *Sherri Benning*

Speaking these words will cause a set of coordinates to be burned
into the skin
- *Kayo Chingonyi*

gun theachd-an-tìr no bhiadh ac'
ach fàileadh ciatach ròs.
- *Alasdair Mac Mhaighstir Alasdair*

Commonplace

No more common,
alive and vital
as the burn's

inflow, the
gutweed-green
submerged stones;

only commonplace,
the unreal
relational lakes

and fields of data,
a waterfall without
water so roaringly

silent in all
its alphanumerical
plunge, scrolling,

scrolling through
a script whose
language spills

over vast catchment
in glittering tributaries—
each string

of patient names
and ages,
end stage

heart failure
and hospital bills
unpaid.

Lichen

Life is blemished and golden
moonglow, a lichen borne of love,
the fruiting body you did not become.
Or did you? We couldn't keep you
hidden in the tussocks of panic
forever, but when you kicked,
fifth instar to a shimmering
green, you were still our little secret.
You quickened into life and through
your mother as she began to darken
with the days: hips to belly button
enclosed a faint line, smile mottled,
a mask cracked into mosaic,
and all during the first trimester.
Too early. I said we're too young.
Never said I was
afraid, but I was. So afraid
I couldn't hear what your mother was
afraid of, this being her one chance.
I didn't see, didn't see
behind surfaces of lichen-grey
overgrowing everything
what you were meant to be: summer's
day-flying butterfly, our mountain ringlet,
rare in your desire for montane air.
Instead you were turned to script lichen,
forked, curved letters no one would believe,
not even me. When the floor
revealed you were bloodspot lichen
I knew what I had done.
Even now, six years since your mother and I

rinsed our fingers clean, I still liken you
to chrysalis, a black word. Black after green,
after regret. The wound death brings
is the afterlife.

Heil Valley

Field run to seed along the grain
of granite, trees under dusk and ruin
complete any piecemeal dark.
Blacker than char, a squirrel angles
toward pitched meadowland, listens
for anything else, an owl
concealed by shadow, or far off,
fast through the canyon that never stops,
the wind-splitter, a motorcycle
dying into night. Nature's sonographer
with big probing ears, it can read sound
as well as hear. Watch how it scans
woodsmoke for a seasonless year
high among the pine-fork, then re-builds
its needle-stitched cup, cache that was
brimful with seed, berry and acorn,
until it realizes nothing
discerns nothing after wildfire, after
the aftermath. Only loss, and worse
the evergreen of memory is reversed
to never-green, a nothing-nest,
so eerily similar to nothingness.

The Bright Field (of Prairie Sunflowers)

That thou canst not stir a flower without troubling a star

— Francis Thompson

I have seen the sun
break over a small field
and break that small field.
Eternity awaits.
As the creator's stare,
obediently held
through midsummer,
intensifies, the created
like sunflowers shrivel:
demands so severe
even the fiercest desert
father would reach
for soft ambivalence.
Relief rather than sin.
Frail leaves of light,
I realize now, are a failure
of prayer, and if I give
to possess,
I only possess failure
and fire like Moses
and the lit bush.

after RS Thomas

The Fetch

over Nebraska
and the high eastern plains
breaks like spindrift
dust swells and the air
itself granulates further
west round this towering
cement island platform
Dry Creek station
cue the empty timpani
from Morricone's main theme
maybe some tumbleweed
because suburbia has been
self-referential ever since
a flag of smog
unfurls over Denver's azure
full-mast wind coruscating
cracks fearless on this
flying day
the interstate roars
toward its vanishing point
at 65 mph no one fears
noise pollution will simplify
birdsong still whistling
Morricone's flutes
luminously delicate
cold sagebrush
susurrates with all birdsong
if only we were listening
if only we could
commuters alight from
the light rail

back to planet Earth and *hush*
commuters must take
no notice at all
I am a commuter
thus I must take
no notice at all

After My Father

Often at work when I'm morning-hours
deep in emails, or done with afternoon
meetings that redefine all meeting rooms,
moments, which I call time's little *hors*

d'oeuvres, dished out delicately as honor,
deliver me to one quite mindless croon,
kicked off by the finger tap of childhood:
desktop drums, interrupting neighbors

and their own metronome of mouse click
and keyboard, the busiest business suite
ever performed, cacophonous yet quiet.

Eyes dilated bright, reading data-music
off monitors so glazed and window-like,
I'm practically jazz inside each moment.

Monday

At a desk whose only windows can be opened on a desktop. I am a voyeur scrolling through the screen when all this time I thought I was a voyager. Spreadsheets, e-mails. I have eyestrain. I take a break, go outside. Third-eye-strain is realizing the high-desert highway I thought was my escape is just higher road through higher desert. I snap out of it, or rather I snap out of nothing, still here, surrounded by golf courses and this whole business of the American dream.

Leelanau

i.m. John Martin

Cherryless orchards uncoil to winter.
Shanties rank with whitefish, the river's
creaky docks. He knew every trap-net tug
by their wakes, long, dwindling epilogues
written across the lake. He would smile,
Ohio State-red dimples below calm
esquire's eyes, watching through the window
their leeward work. His error and wound:
Leelanau was 'delight of life'… He half-
laughed knowing how often lake turns to lack
and takes after the sky after the sky
turns grey, after the Great Lake freighters ply
January, whose second, greater blank
outgrew the pane in which he saw himself.

Leelanau (Again)

for my wife

Let us journey further north
than midsummer, across this bright rising
peninsula, borderless
almost in identity
it negotiates province and promise,
an Algonquian state that shares
deep in the understory
of sweet woodruff
a secret rediscovery,
just when we thought there was little left
to know and too much to bear. We'll not bear it
alone. We'll not dare.
Let's return, share this first truce,
as Michigan and Huron tremendously cleave
and by the mere hyphen of Mackinac
straits become one.
Love is a hyphen. Let us draw on
love that serves
rather than severs. We'll follow through
Kalm's St John's Wort
brushing our ankles,
nearly traceless in our place, like pollen dust
fallen off the rarest purple martin.

@RestAndBeThankful

                                    Why work
when folding my laptop, clasped as a briefcase,
relieves both eyes at once? The eleventh hour,
despite all talk of being equal, renders the most dutiful
a dunce whose thinking cap is his head, and his head
he unfolds five days a week, eight hours a day—

       except for yesterday, and yesteryear,
       except for his boss, and his boss' boss,
       except for SQL queries that never quite pull
       enough data from the not-for-profit warehouse
       of pipe-delimited fields.

I'd be first to retire penniless
if it meant happiness at last.
It doesn't. Get on with it,
calendar-boy! Time breaks
into quadrants—days, months, quarters.
Each a square nested within a square.
All my life I've been taught
to think outside the box,
only to learn that wisdom itself
has four walls, and on weekends
I can have my home office,
my whole mancave, ordered by author.

First-world dilemma, dude;
you dismiss it, in vain. For we are all
complainants, no matter this world or that,
though grass is always greener where it rains
nonstop, off the A83 and highest hill.
Geotag me @RestAndBeThankful.

As one of the smitmarked herd, hefted to wet turf,
I'll keep hunched over like a question mark,
grassy muzzle causing landslips
for which I'll be blamed,
no less displaced, even here
the slopes are overgrazed.
Glacial debris, mica schists
like rain, ruin the viewpoints
which drover and driver
work to maintain.

Alba, Or Scotland, No Black Coffee Will Help

my whiteboy misery at three am:
stubbornly trying to turn a sonnet
into visa-speak, that sass of Home
Office. What is 'exceptional talent'?
Calvin Harris-bass drops? Rihanna-rhyme?
The flashlight & fast life of Kanye West?
It's three am,
                    Alba.

                              Too late to sing
how our pointed borders are pointless
in love. They cleave, sever all thistle
& laughter & you are Lady Gaga's
chart-topping mezzo-mania.
If I were Bradley Cooper's sixstring,
or Cash Warren's westcoast smile,
maybe I'd marry my Jessica Alba.

ImmRAM

Skip the birdshit & black glowering sky,
klaxon horn & the brine
for clean landing pages—islands cherrypicked
by your own double-click,
a rainbow pinwheel spinning.

                          Imagine

machine code, all apps open, *peregrinatio 2.0*:
your shrineless arrival,
your sojourn never begun,
feather-clipped by search results.

Passengers

Winter moon ripening.
We bellyache of cold,
huddled outside the cèilidh
like penguins.
Everyone has holidayed home,
eyes bright as Christmas lights,
but will ferry away tomorrow
determined
to hop on/hop off each year
and each island
just to stay ahead of home,
us included.

Our bus arrives.
A star across midnight dives

then vanishes. Passengers,
all of us, talk of how the dark is
marvelous, how it has
a counterbalance of moon and stars
some nights.
Some nights it doesn't.

Nine Whales, Tiree

Walking, walking through morning thaw,
the melon-light dripping from each rock
like meltwater, and he wonders how

night will ever fall again over Tiree
surprised by the ruins that come with day:
bonehouses huge, haunted, creak,

shaped to the bends and the bight of bay.
Though hollowed they refill with light.
Though brilliant they are abandoned.

May Day

Antrim swam the mist and distance over faded sea-greys as we
lingered up the steeper bealach to the north. The land was horned,
its granite tusk spearheaded the heavens: a dark fraying rain, burning
off ridge after ridge. Light uncoiled along the deer fence for miles
the way need-fire used to purify this glen before it was cleared. Why
else had we come? Not to summit the pinnacle so much as to stand
there and mirror it. Light illuminated granite. We paused beside its
natural prayer to rest, shielded beneath the peak. Gorgeous coarse
granite, pocketed and split clean. We pressed barehanded against
the slabs. We listened to shrinking and cracking patterns, to trilled
silences of wind and air—earth's striated surface speaking through
parallels in our palm lines, pink with cold. Confessions of granite:
trustworthy when dry, and as slick as ice when wet. Sharing the
shoulder weight, one pack between us, we journeyed just shy of the
sky and everywhere within.

The Low Road

…toward the chamber of darkness, winter, death.
— George Mackay Brown

Peewits excitedly sing, 'Come and listen
with a father's ear.' My head pressed to her
belly, swollen with renewal. I dream
we are pregnant again, sharing the same
green among grey, the selfsame startled heart
that Maeshowe, like the navel of the north,
offers at first glance. We couldn't keep it
for our own reasons, reasons all our own;
but when you resolve to take this low road
you cannot stall or take it back. Maeshowe,
soft and runic, the valley's womb-ruin—
an innermost chambered dark through which
sightseers and walkers-between-worlds,
like angels, thread one peerie, final light.

Theneva at Culross

                          the world tilted
      toward a pink ring   but night
        held dominance
                          as I walked
        up to my thighs
            in iciest cold   bladderwrack
        at every knuckle   kissed and licked clean
            my fingertips   from which
        salty water-stars   had trembled

    and I waded deeper
                          a shiver   blood freezes
      expands into bruises   like green secrets
      at such temperatures   I craved to be
                submerged   trapped in the wintertidal
          its estuary trick   stung my lungs
            with salt and   became a dream
            unbuttoning   you again

      you rumored me   a darkness I had to flee
                          on an oarless raft
    the frailest wickerwork
        if only to discover
                          I was carrying

    those who received me   ears chill
              on my belly   claimed to hear
          the firth swell   but I was skeptical
          rather than oil   my son was embalmed
              in legend   said to skyre
    like a stained-glass saint

                              and out of fear

                for his soul
        they stole his memory   I lost everything

      the bed you and I shared   the blame
            we should've shared   everything
            I waded into night   to feel

        the bottom drop
        yet found myself
      cowled with water   unbraided hair
catching in the tangle   of what was

Prayer

after Alasdair Mac Mhaighstir Alasdair

God bless
this sea-vessel,

which from the very first day,
it seems, was shouldered
by Clanranald. Lowered to the bay,
our war-torn heroes are heroes
beyond war, beyond the gale
and the ghost-note of air;
far out beyond incisive breakers
shattering over a rocky shore,

may you, sacred
cubed God,

harbour us, moor us to the hush.
It was you flooded earth
and pressed into cardinal points
a compass of wind that skirls
after all. So keep us, father,
our kyle-slicer and steel,
craft and crew, in your safekeep.
Sails, rigging, anchor, rudder.

Fix our tackle
like your only son

to the mast, a seaborne crucifix,
and each mast-ring also
that secures the sail-yards and all
the moss-fir and heather ropes

be blessed: halyard and stay
flawless as you refuse us
our failure, our drift off-course.
Cartographer of every berth

      under the sun, we bask
      in your direction.

Dundee

Patterns of ashlar, slate. The gable-fronts
gather round in hard shadows and one by one
parked cars, the streets. All are gathered up.

Soft chevrons of white and ashen snow
soundproof this city. I collapse, a drunk
bundled in night, my buttonless greatcoat.

Fingal's Address to Oscar

after Ossian

Grandson, you are prince to first heroes.
I saw the glint of your sword,
and the gratitude it composed
in me: your coda of war.
But remember each ancestor's
great footsteps, and walk within them.

When they lived—Trenmor
and Trathull, both fathers-at-arms—
every battle had a champion,
and they were champions at battle.
Their names crescendo from now on
in poetry's old ensemble.

So go, Oscar, quash any conqueror.
But raise up all others mercifully.

Winter's torrent, spring's meltwater.
Be either force against our enemies.
Be also soft breeze, summer zephyr.
To all in need, you are wanted relief.
Like Trathull or Trenmor, even me,
to this, you have lent a hand
with warm welcome. Grandson,

here, take heart and home
beneath the starlight of my sword.

for my Grandfather

The Air Debris

after Don Paterson

,   ;
,   ;
                    ?
              ,

                        ?
                  ?
                    ,
                              ,
        ,   ,
                    ?
              ?
    ,   ?

Acknowledgements

Thanks to the outlets in which some of these poems first appeared: *The New Statesman, Times Literary Supplement, Poetry Review, The Dark Horse Magazine, New Writing Scotland, Northwords Now, The London Magazine, December Magazine, Magma, The Interpreter's House, Orbis,* and *The Lincoln Review.*

Thanks to so many who have helped me plod my pen a little less. My wife, for trusting me, my whole family, and in particular my father, who reads everything I write; friends and guidance, Kevin Barnes, Tristram Colledge, Miguel F Dos Santos, Matt Schmidt, Ryan Lindner, Eilidh NicAonghais, Deb Marber, Nick Hughes, Torcuil Grant, Niall Campbell, Seán Hewitt, David George Haskell, David Nichols, Pierre Antoine, Jack McGowan, Brian Kearney, Ryann Ferguson Durie, Alan Riach, James Adam Shelley, Gillebrìde MacMillan, Claire Kennedy, Jen Hadfield, David Wheatley, Anna Crowe, Isabel Galleymore, Sarah Stewart, Jane McKie, Kristi Harvey, Don Paterson, John Burnside, Jacob Polley, Jay Hopler, Karen Brown, and for the first writer to believe in me, Daniele Pantano. (No doubt other names could be included.)

Thanks to my editor Aaron Kent and to the whole Broken Sleep family.

Thanks lastly to Olivia Booker and Fee Blumenthaler for lifting *Nine Whales* off the page and putting it onto the big screen.

LAY OUT YOUR UNREST

Milton Keynes UK
Ingram Content Group UK Ltd.
UKHW040953050923
428080UK00004B/93